Beginning React

Simplify your frontend development workflow and enhance the user experience of your applications with React

Andrea Chiarelli

BIRMINGHAM - MUMBAI

Beginning React

Acquisitions Editor: Koushik Sen
Content Development Editors: Tanmayee Patil, Taabish Khan
Production Coordinator: Ratan Pote

First published: July 2018

Production reference: 1250718

Published by Packt Publishing Ltd.
Livery Place
35 Livery Street
Birmingham
B3 2PB, UK.

ISBN 978-1-78953-052-0

www.packtpub.com

`mapt.io`

Mapt is an online digital library that gives you full access to over 5,000 books and videos, as well as industry leading tools to help you plan your personal development and advance your career. For more information, please visit our website.

Why Subscribe?

- Spend less time learning and more time coding with practical eBooks and Videos from over 4,000 industry professionals
- Improve your learning with Skill Plans built especially for you
- Get a free eBook or video every month
- Mapt is fully searchable
- Copy and paste, print, and bookmark content

PacktPub.com

Did you know that Packt offers eBook versions of every book published, with PDF and ePub files available? You can upgrade to the eBook version at `www.PacktPub.com` and as a print book customer, you are entitled to a discount on the eBook copy. Get in touch with us at `service@packtpub.com` for more details.

At `www.PacktPub.com`, you can also read a collection of free technical articles, sign up for a range of free newsletters, and receive exclusive discounts and offers on Packt books and eBooks.

Contributors

About the Author

Andrea Chiarelli has over 20 years of experience as a software engineer and technical writer. In his professional career, he has used various technologies for his projects: from C# to JavaScript, from Angular to React, and ASP.NET to PhoneGap/Cordova. He has contributed to many online and offline magazines and is the author of several books published by Wrox Press and Packt. Currently, he is a software architect at the Italian office of Apparound, Inc. and a regular contributor to HTML.it, an Italian online magazine focused on web technologies.

I wish to thank my family for their support, patience, and love.

About the Reviewer

Graeme Wolfendale is a software engineer. He has used a range of tools in his line of work, mostly focusing on frontend web technologies such as JavaScript, HTML, and CSS, alongside backend PHP/C#. He enjoys writing code on both the frontend and backend, as well as interacting with third-party APIs. Currently, he works as a software engineer at n-Coders Limited, a software company that specializes in bespoke web app development.

Packt Is Searching for Authors like You

If you're interested in becoming an author for Packt, please visit `authors.packtpub.com` and apply today. We have worked with thousands of developers and tech professionals, just like you, to help them share their insight with the global tech community. You can make a general application, apply for a specific hot topic that we are recruiting an author for, or submit your own idea.

Table of Contents

Preface

Projects like Angular and React are rapidly changing how development teams build and deploy web applications to production. In this book, you'll learn the basics you need to get up and running with React and tackle real-world projects and challenges. The book includes helpful guidance on how to consider key user requirements within the development process, and also shows you how to work with advanced concepts such as state management, data-binding, routing, and the popular component markup that is JSX. As you complete the included examples you'll find yourself well-equipped to move onto a real-world personal or professional frontend project.

After completing this book, you will be able to:

- Understand how React works within a wider application stack
- Analyze how you can break down a standard interface into specific components
- Successfully create your own increasingly complex React components with HTML or JSX
- Correctly handle multiple user events and their impact on overall application state
- Understand the component lifecycle to optimize the UX of your application
- Configure routing to allow effortless, intuitive navigation through your components

Who This Book Is For

If you are a frontend developer who wants to create truly reactive user interfaces in JavaScript, then this the book for you. For React, you'll need a solid foundation in the essentials of the JavaScript language, including new OOP features that were introduced in ES2015. An understanding of HTML and CSS is assumed, and a basic knowledge of Node.js will be useful in the context of managing a development workflow, but is not essential.

What This Book Covers

Chapter 1, *Introducing React and UI Design*, introduces React and helps us to start building the basic infrastructure of a React-based application. Then, we will analyze how to design a user interface so that it can be easily mapped to React components.

Chapter 2, *Creating Components*, teaches us how to implement React components, how to assemble multiple components into one, and how to manage their internal states. We will explore React component implementation by building a simple application.

Chapter 3, *Managing User Interactivity*, teaches us how to manage the events generated by a user's interaction with the components of a React-based user interface. We will explore the events that are triggered during the lifecycle of a React component, and will learn how to exploit them in order to create efficient components.

To Get the Most out of This Book

This book will require a system with the following minimum hardware requirements:

- Processor: Pentium 4 (or equivalent)
- 4 GB RAM
- Hard disk space: 10 GB
- An internet connection

The following software should also be installed:

- Any modern operating system (preferably, Windows 10 version 1507)
- The latest version of Node.js (https://nodejs.org/en/)
- The latest version of any modern browser (preferably, Chrome)

Download the Example Code Files

You can download the example code files for this book from your account at www.packtpub.com. If you purchased this book elsewhere, you can visit www.packtpub.com/support and register to have the files emailed directly to you.

You can download the code files by following these steps:

1. Log in or register at www.packtpub.com.
2. Select the **SUPPORT** tab.
3. Click on **Code Downloads & Errata**.
4. Enter the name of the book in the **Search** box and follow the onscreen instructions.

Once the file is downloaded, please make sure that you unzip or extract the folder using the latest version of:

- WinRAR/7-Zip for Windows
- Zipeg/iZip/UnRarX for Mac
- 7-Zip/PeaZip for Linux

The code bundle for the book is also hosted on GitHub at `https://github.com/ TrainingByPackt/Beginning-React`. In case there's an update to the code, it will be updated on the existing GitHub repository.

We also have other code bundles from our rich catalog of books and videos available at `https://github.com/PacktPublishing/`. Check them out!

Download the Color Images

We also provide a PDF file that has color images of the screenshots/diagrams used in this book. You can download it here: `https://www.packtpub.com/sites/default/files/ downloads/BeginningReact_ColorImages.pdf`.

Conventions Used

There are a number of text conventions used throughout this book.

`CodeInText`: Indicates code words in text, database table names, folder names, filenames, file extensions, pathnames, dummy URLs, user input, and Twitter handles. Here is an example: "By wrapping the `App` component, the `BrowserRouter` component enriches it with routing capabilities."

A block of code is set as follows:

```
class Catalog extends React.Component {
  constructor() {
    super();
```

When we wish to draw your attention to a particular part of a code block, the relevant lines or items are set in bold:

```
import { BrowserRouter } from 'react-router-dom'
ReactDOM.render(
  <BrowserRouter>
    <App />
  </BrowserRouter>
  , document.getElementById('root'));
```

Any command-line input or output is written as follows:

```
create-react-app --version
```

Bold: Indicates a new term, an important word, or words that you see onscreen. For example, words in menus or dialog boxes appear in the text like this. Here is an example: "Now we need to create a view to display the **Catalog** component or the **About** page."

Activity: These are scenario-based activities that will let you practically apply what you've learned over the course of a complete section. They are typically in the context of a real-world problem or situation.

 Warnings or important notes appear like this.

Get in Touch

Feedback from our readers is always welcome.

General feedback: Email feedback@packtpub.com and mention the book title in the subject of your message. If you have questions about any aspect of this book, please email us at questions@packtpub.com.

Errata: Although we have taken every care to ensure the accuracy of our content, mistakes do happen. If you have found a mistake in this book, we would be grateful if you would report this to us. Please visit www.packtpub.com/submit-errata, selecting your book, clicking on the Errata Submission Form link, and entering the details.

Piracy: If you come across any illegal copies of our works in any form on the Internet, we would be grateful if you would provide us with the location address or website name. Please contact us at copyright@packtpub.com with a link to the material.

If you are interested in becoming an author: If there is a topic that you have expertise in and you are interested in either writing or contributing to a book, please visit `authors.packtpub.com`.

Reviews

Please leave a review. Once you have read and used this book, why not leave a review on the site that you purchased it from? Potential readers can then see and use your unbiased opinion to make purchase decisions, we at Packt can understand what you think about our products, and our authors can see your feedback on their book. Thank you!

For more information about Packt, please visit `packtpub.com`.

Introducing React and UI Design

1

React is definitely one of the most talked about libraries on the web. It has become as popular as jQuery was in its prime, and more and more developers choose it to build the user interface of their web applications. Why has it become so popular? Why is this JavaScript library so innovative compared to others?

We will try to provide answers to these questions in this book by showing what the library offers, and by using it to build efficient web user interfaces.

In this chapter, we will introduce React and we will start building the basic infrastructure of a React-based application. Then, we will analyze how to design a user interface so that it can be easily mapped to React components, exploiting the best from React's internal architecture.

By the end of this chapter, you will be able to:

- Describe what React is and where it fits in the development of your applications
- Set up the infrastructure of a React-based application
- Design the UI of your application, optimizing it for use in React

What is React?

To put it simply, React is a JavaScript library for building composable user interfaces. This means that we can build a user interface by composing items called **components**. A component is an element that contributes to building a user interface. It could be a textbox, a button, a whole form, a group of other components, and so on. Even the entire application's user interface is a component. So, React encourages the creation of components to build a user interface; it's even better if these components are reusable.

React components have the ability to present data that changes over time, and the visualization of that changing data is automatic when we follow a few guidelines.

Since the library deals with user interfaces, you may wonder which presentational design patterns React was inspired by: **Model-View-Controller**, **Model-View-Presenter**, **Model-View-ViewModel**, or something else. React is not bound to a specific presentational pattern. React implements the *View* part of the most common patterns, leaving developers free to choose the best approach to implement the model, the presenter, and everything else they need to build their application. This aspect is important, since it allows us to classify it as a library, not as a framework; therefore, comparisons with frameworks such as Angular may throw up some inconsistencies.

How to Set up a React-Based Application

React is a JavaScript library, so we should be able to make a reference to it through a `<script>` tag in our HTML page and start writing our web application. However, this approach would prevent us from exploiting some features that are provided by a modern JavaScript development environment—features that make our lives easier. For example, we wouldn't be able to use recent features from ECMAScript 2015+, such as classes, modules, arrow functions, `let` and `const` statements, and so on. Or, we could use those features, but only recent browsers would support them.

The relationship of ECMAScript with JavaScript

Using the latest ECMAScript features requires a true development environment, allowing us to transpile our code into ECMAScript 5 version JavaScript code, so that even older browsers will be able to run our application. Setting up a modern JavaScript development environment requires the installation and configuration of a few tools: a transpiler, a syntax checker, a module bundler, a task runner, and so on. Learning to use these tools properly requires a lot of time, even before starting to write a single line of code.

Installing create-react-app

Fortunately, we can use `create-react-app`, a **command-line interface (CLI)** tool that allows us to set up a React-based application without needing to configure any of the aforementioned tools. It is based on Node.js and provides commands to set up and modify a React application in an immediate way.

In order to install `create-react-app`, you need Node.js installed on your machine. You can install the CLI by typing the following command in a console window:

```
npm install -g create-react-app
```

After installation, you can verify whether it is properly installed by typing the following command:

```
create-react-app --version
```

If all is OK, the installed version of `create-react-app` will be shown.

Creating Your First React Application

Now that the development environment is installed, let's create our first React application. We can do this by typing the following command in a console window:

```
create-react-app hello-react
```

This command tells `create-react-app` to set up all of the prerequisites for a React-based application named `hello-react`. The creation process may take several minutes, since it has to download the npm packages needed for the project.

 npm is the standard package manager of the Node.js environment. When the process ends, you will find a list of the available commands that you can run to manage the project on the screen. We will return to this later. The result of the project creation will be a folder named `hello-react`, inside of which you will find the items composing a dummy—but working—React-based application.

Activity: Creating an Application with create-react-app

Scenario

We need to set up a development environment in order to create a product catalog application built with React.

Aim

The aim of the activity is to start becoming familiar with `create-react-app` and the content it creates.

Steps for Completion

1. Use `create-react-app` to create the development environment
2. Give the name `my-shop` to the sample application

Solution

There is no formal solution. You should focus on the content created by `create-react-app`, as we are going to analyze it in the following sections.

Exploring the Generated Content

Let's take a look at the files generated by `create-react-app`, so that we can get an understanding of the structure of a React-based application. We will find these files and folders inside of the `HELLO-REACT` folder as shown in the following screenshot:

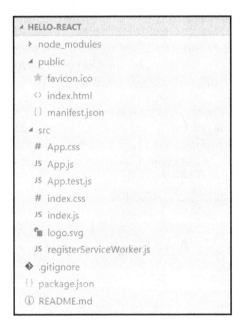

In the root folder, we can see a `README.md` file, the `package.json` file, and the `.gitignore` file.

The `README` document contains references to all you need to start building a React-based application. It is written in Markdown format, and you can integrate or overwrite it with your own documentation.

Markdown is a simple markup language, often used to create technical documentation for software libraries. It requires a simple text editor, and it is possible to convert a Markdown document into HTML.

The `package.json` file contains information about the project, such as the name, the version, and so on, and references to all the npm packages used by the current project. This is a Node.js asset that allows you to download the required packages when copying the project to another machine. It also contains the definitions of scripts that allow us to manage the project itself.

The following is an example of `package.json` file content:

```
{
  "name": "hello-react",
  "version": "0.1.0",
  "private": true,
  "dependencies": {
    "react": "^16.0.0",
    "react-dom": "^16.0.0",
    "react-scripts": "1.0.14"
  },
  "scripts": {
    "start": "react-scripts start",
    "build": "react-scripts build",
    "test": "react-scripts test --env=jsdom",
    "eject": "react-scripts eject"
  }
}
```

As we can see, the file's content is a JSON object, with a few easy to recognize properties. In particular, we can identify the project's name, the version, and package dependencies. Apart from the name and version properties, usually, you don't need to manually change these settings.

The `.gitignore` file is a hidden file in Unix-based systems, and it allows us to track which file(s) to ignore when using Git as a version control system. The `create-react-app` tool added this file because nowadays, it is essential to have a project under version control. It suggests Git, since it is one of the most popular version control systems.

The `public` folder contains the static parts of our application:

- `favicon`: This is the icon shown in the browser's address bar and is used for bookmarks

- `index.html`: This is the HTML page containing the reference to our React code and providing a context to React rendering
- `manifest.json`: This is a configuration file containing metadata according to the **Progressive Web Apps (PWA)** criteria

In particular, the `index.html` file is the starting point of our application. Let's take a look at it so that we can understand what's special about it:

```
<!doctype html>
<html lang="en">
  <head>
    <meta charset="utf-8">
    <meta name="viewport" content="width=device-width, initial-scale=1,
shrink-to-fit=no">
    <meta name="theme-color" content="#000000">
    <link rel="manifest" href="%PUBLIC_URL%/manifest.json">
...
    <title>React App</title>
  </head>
  <body>
    <noscript>
      You need to enable JavaScript to run this app.
    </noscript>
  <div id="root"></div>
...
</html>
```

As we can see, it is a standard HTML page; however, a few things should be noted. First of all, we see a link to the `manifest.json` file:

```
<link rel="manifest" href="%PUBLIC_URL%/manifest.json">
```

This manifest contains metadata for configuring our app as a PWA.

 Progressive web apps are web applications that work for every browser and every platform, even offline. Their basic tenet is responsiveness and progressive enhancement.

The second thing we notice is the `%PUBLIC_URL%` placeholder in both link references:

```
<link rel="manifest" href="%PUBLIC_URL%/manifest.json">
<link rel="shortcut icon" href="%PUBLIC_URL%/favicon.ico">
```

This placeholder will be replaced with the actual URL of the `public` folder during the build process.

The body of the HTML page contains an empty `div` with a root identifier. This is an important item for the correct setup of our React application, as we will soon see. Apart from the `<noscript>` tag, we do not see any other element in the body. However, we need a binding between the HTML page and the JavaScript. The build process will be responsible for adding the required scripts to the body.

 We can add any other required items to the HTML page, such as meta tags, web fonts, and so on. However, remember that files referenced inside the HTML markup should be put in the `public` folder. The `node_modules` folder contains the npm packages used by the project. Usually, you don't need to directly manage these files.

The most important folder for developing our application is the `src` folder. It contains the basic files, with the code that we can modify for our purposes.

In particular, we will find the following files:

- `index.js`: Contains the starting point of our application
- `index.css`: Stores the base styling for our application
- `App.js`: Contains the definition of the main component of the sample application
- `App.css`: Contains the styling of the `App` component
- `logo.svg`: This is the React logo
- `App.test.js`: Stores the basic unit test involving the `App` component
- `registerServiceWorker.js`: Contains the code to register the service worker in order to allow offline behavior, as per the PWA requirements

Let's analyze the content of a couple of these files, since their code is fundamental to understanding how the startup of a React application works.

Let's start with the `index.js` file. Its content is shown as follows:

```
import React from 'react';
import ReactDOM from 'react-dom';
import './index.css';
import App from './App';
import registerServiceWorker from './registerServiceWorker';

ReactDOM.render(<App />, document.getElementById('root'));
registerServiceWorker();
```

It is an ECMAScript 2015 module, importing other modules. In particular, it imports the `React` and `ReactDOM` objects from the `react` and `react-dom` modules, respectively. Both modules are part of the React library and are stored inside the `node_modules` folder.

The `react` module provides functionality for component creation and state management. The `react-dom` module is the glue between React components and the HTML DOM. The React library has been split into two modules in order to separate the component management from the actual rendering. This separation may be useful when we want to target a rendering platform that is not the web; for example, if we want to target native mobile rendering.

Other modules are imported from the same folder as the `index.js` file. In particular, we import the `App` component from the `App` module. The `App` component is used by the `render()` method of the `ReactDOM` object in order to bind it to the `div` element in the HTML page. This magic is performed by the following statement:

```
ReactDOM.render(<App />, document.getElementById('root'));
```

For the moment, let's ignore the syntax used to render the `App` component. This will be covered in the next chapter. The meaning of this statement is to associate the React `App` component defined inside the `App` module with the HTML element identified by the `root` ID.

The `registerServiceWorker()` function import and invocation enables the support for offline behavior, in line with the PWA specification, while the import of `index.css` makes the CSS styling available to the application.

The `App.js` file contains the definition of the React component representing the application. Its content looks like the following:

```
import React, { Component } from 'react';
import logo from './logo.svg';
import './App.css';

class App extends Component {
  render() {
    return (
      <div className="App">
        <header className="App-header">
          <img src={logo} className="App-logo" alt="logo" />
          <h1 className="App-title">Welcome to React</h1>
        </header>
        <p className="App-intro">
...
export default App;
```

Let's take a quick look at the code, since it will be covered in detail in the next chapter. For the moment, we only want to get a very basic idea of how a React component is defined. Here, we see a module importing a few items from other modules, defining the App class by inheriting from the Component class and exporting the App class itself as a default export. That's all, for the moment. We will cover this code in depth in the next chapter, understanding its meaning in detail.

The create-react-app Commands

The create-react-app CLI provides a few commands to manage our React project. These commands appear in the form npm <command>, since they are based on the npm.

 If you prefer to use YARN as a package manager, you should replace yarn wherever you find npm.

The npm start Command

The first command we will cover is npm start. This command starts a development web server accepting requests at http://localhost:3000.

So, after launching this command, we can open a browser and see the following result:

The development web server has a hot reloading system that allows us to change the code of our application and get the page refreshed in the browser after saving the file.

Changing File Content and Viewing the Result

This following steps show how changing the content of a file causes the application to reload in the browser:

1. Open a console window.
2. Go to the `hello-react` folder.
3. Run `npm start`.
4. Launch a browser and go to `http://localhost:3000`.
5. Launch a text editor and open the `App.js` file.
6. Search for the following line of code:

   ```
   To get started, edit <code>src/App.js</code> and save to reload.
   ```

7. Replace the code mentioned in step 6 with the following line of code:

   ```
   Hello React!
   ```

8. Save the file.
9. Check the browser content. Now it should display the new text.

Activity: Starting and Changing the Application

Scenario

We want to change the title of the application that was created in the previous activity.

Aim

The aim of the activity is to become familiar with launching an application and appreciating the hot reloading feature.

Steps for Completion

1. Start the application so that you can see it in a browser
2. Edit the `App.js` file and set the title to `My Shop`

Solution

There is no formal solution. You should focus on getting the title correctly changed and the application running.

The npm test Command

`create-react-app` promotes the use of unit tests by generating a sample unit test file, as we have already seen, and by providing a set of tools to run such tests.

These tools are based on **Jest**, and we can run the tests written within our application by running the following command:

```
npm test
```

This command will start running our test and will show the results, as shown in the following screenshot:

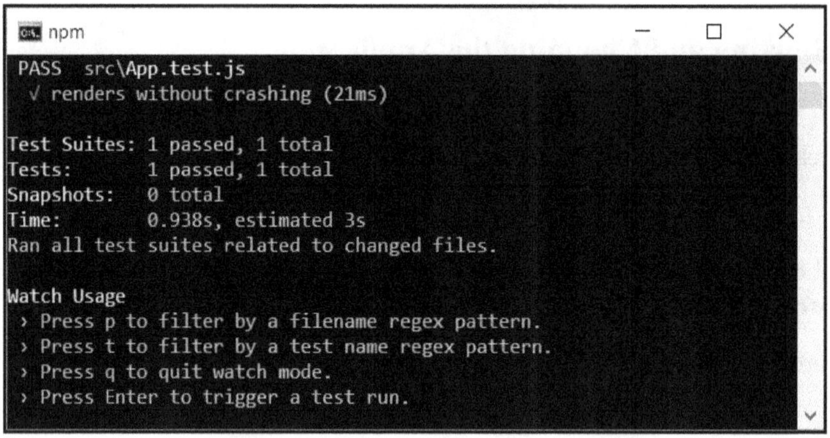

The npm run build Command

When we are ready to move our application into the production environment, we need the artifacts to publish. We can produce these artifacts by running the following command:

```
npm run build
```

The result of running this command is a new BUILD folder where we will find all of the files that we need to move into a production environment. The command carries out some processing on the files of our development environment. Put simply, it translates all of the ES2015 code we wrote into ES5 compatible code, so that it is also available for older browsers. This process is called **transpilation**. In addition, it reduces the size of the code itself, allowing for faster downloading over the network. This process is called **minification**. Finally, it takes the files in our development environment and combines them into a few files, called bundles, in order to decrease network requests.

The following screenshot shows the content of the BUILD folder of the sample application:

To publish the production build of our application, we can just copy the content of the BUILD folder into the production server's folder.

The result of the production build assumes that the artifact will be published into the web server root, that is, at a location where the application will be accessible through a URL such as http://www.myapplication.com.

If we need to publish the application in a root's subfolder, that is, at a location where the application will be accessible through a URL such as http://www.myapplication.com/app, we need to make a slight change to the package.json file.

In this case, we need to add a homepage key to the configuration JSON with the URL as its value, as shown here:
"homepage": "http://www.myapplication.com/app".

The npm run eject Command

The last command we will cover is the `eject` command:

```
npm run eject
```

We can use this command when we are confident in using the tools underlying `create-react-app` and we need to customize the environment configuration. This command takes our application out of the CLI context and gives us the power and responsibility to manage it.

 This is a one-way process. If we leave the `create-react-app` context for our application, we cannot go back.

How to Design a UI

Now, we are going to see how we can design our application so that it fits well when implemented with React.

Everything Is a Component

The main concept introduced by React in user interface design and implementation is the component concept. A user interface is an aggregate of components, and the whole React application is an aggregate of components. We will now see in more detail what components are from a design point of view.

 From a design point of view, we can say that a component is a part of the user interface, having a specific role. A hierarchy of components is often called a component tree.

Consider a form in a web page. It can be treated as a component, since it has a specific role: to collect data and send it to the server. Also, a textbox inside the form can be considered a component. It has a specific role: to collect a single piece of data that will be sent to the server. So, a component may contain other components. And this is what usually happens: a user interface is a hierarchy of components, where some components contain other components.

Keep this concept in mind, since it will be useful to implement efficient and reusable user interfaces.

Decompose a User Interface

To better understand how to design a user interface and how to create components to implement them, we will try to decompose a well-known web user interface—the YouTube main page:

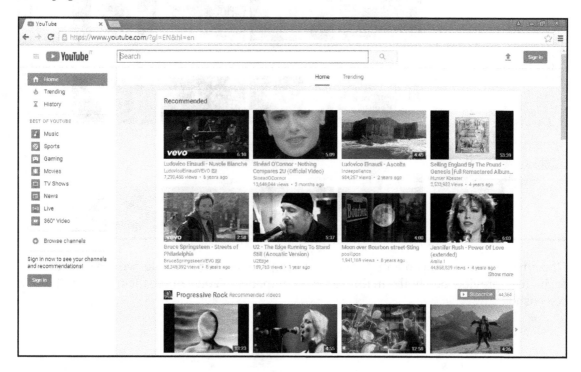

We can detect several items on this page, each having a specific role, starting with the page itself, whose role is to allow the user to interact with the system.

If we consider the header, the left sidebar, and the main area, all of these items are components of the page. You can see them highlighted in the following screenshot:

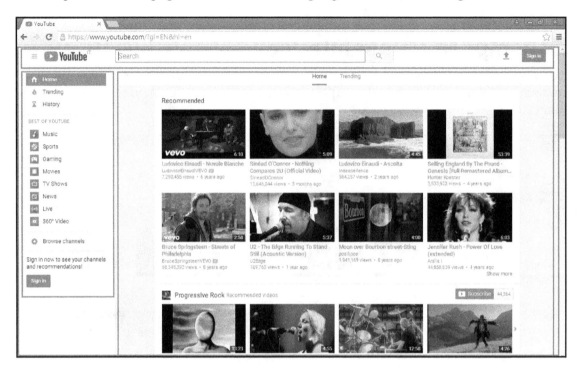

Of course, we can go ahead and detect other components. For example, we can consider each video preview box in the main area as a component. You can see them in the following screenshot:

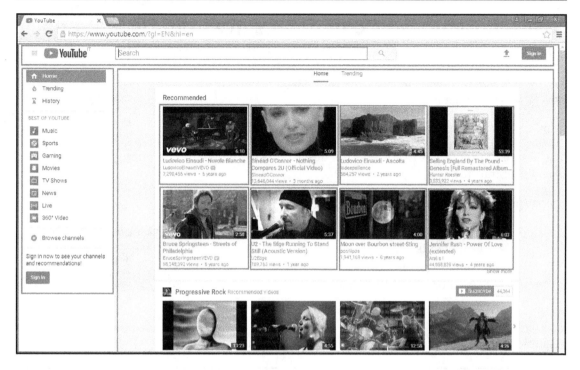

This decomposition process allows us to focus on the specific role of each item in an interface, so that we can try to isolate each functionality and create reusable components, that is, components with just the dependencies that really matter.

Container and Presentational Components

We can classify the components in a user interface into container and presentational components.

The container components are components that do not have a relevant visual effect. Their main role is to group other components, that is, *contain* other components. For example, a form is usually a container component, since its main role is to contain other components, such as textboxes, labels, buttons, and so on.

The presentational components are components that display data in some graphical form. A textbox, a date picker, and a toolbar are examples of presentational components.

The distinction between container and presentational components is very important in order to create efficient user interfaces in React. We will exploit this distinction later, when we learn to manage the components' state and to propagate data through the components.

Activity: Detecting Components in a Web User Interface

Scenario

We need to convert the Wikipedia website's user interface (`https://en.wikipedia.org`) into React components.

Aim

The aim of the activity is to address the design process when implementing React-based user interfaces.

Steps for Completion

1. Analyze the page's current structure and detect the items you can implement as components
2. Indicate which would be container and which would be presentational components

Solution

Assume that the following is the current Wikipedia home page:

A possible solution could be as follows.

We can detect the following components:

- The *home page* component contains the *left sidebar* component, the *header* component, and the *main area* component. All of these components are container components.
- The *left-side* component contains the *logo* component (presentational) and a list of *section* components (presentational).
- The *header* component contains a list of *link* components (presentational) to general pieces of functionality.
- The *main area* component contains a list of *tab* components (container) and a *search* component (presentational).
- The main *tab* component contains a *banner* component (presentational), a *topic index* component (presentational), and a list of *block* components (presentational).

Summary

In this chapter, we started to explore the React world. In particular, we:

- Established that React is a user interface library, used to implement the View part of various MV* design patterns
- Introduced the `create-react-app` tool, which helps us to set up a development environment to build React-based applications
- Explored the items composing a typical React-based application
- Analyzed the approach to designing user interfaces that best fits in the React world

In the next chapter, we will discover how to create React components to build user interfaces for our application.

2
Creating Components

In this chapter, we are going to learn how to implement React components, how to assemble multiple components into one, and how to manage their internal states. We will explore React component implementation by building a simple application. This application will be implemented step-by-step, in order to put the outlined concepts into practice.

By the end of this chapter, you will be able to:

- Create basic React components
- Use JSX to define a component's markup
- Combine multiple React components in order to create complex UI elements
- Manage the internal state of React components

Definition of a Component

As defined in the previous chapter, components are the fundamental building blocks of React. Virtually any visual item in a user interface can be a component. From a formal point of view, we would say that a React component is a piece of JavaScript code defining a portion of a user interface.

Consider the following code in a file:

```
import React from 'react';

class Catalog extends React.Component {
  render() {
    return <div><h2>Catalog</h2></div>;
  }
}

export default Catalog;
```

This is an ECMAScript 2015 module, defining a basic React component.

It imports the `React` namespace from the `react` module and defines the `Catalog` class by extending the `React.Component` class. The module exports the `Catalog` class as a default export.

The interesting part of this definition is the implementation of the `render()` method.

The `render()` method defines the visual part of the component. It may execute any JavaScript code, and it should return a markup expression defining its visual output. The presence of the `render()` method is mandatory for React components. In our example, the `render()` method returns the following markup:

```
<div><h2>Catalog</h2></div>
```

It looks like HTML; although it uses similar syntax, it defines plain objects called **elements**. React elements are similar to **Document Object Model (DOM)** elements, but are lighter and more efficient. So, React components generate a set of React elements that will be mapped to DOM elements by the library's engine. This set of React elements is called the **Virtual DOM**, a lightweight representation of the browser's DOM. React takes care of updating the DOM to match the Virtual DOM, only when it is strictly necessary. This approach allows React to have very high performance when rendering user interfaces.

The `render()` method must comply with a few constraints:

- It is mandatory; that is, every React component must implement it
- It must return one React element; that is, a single markup item with any nested elements
- It should be a pure function; that is, it should not change the internal state of the component (we will discuss this topic in further detail in the next section)
- It should not directly interact with the browser; that is, it shouldn't contain statements that try to access the DOM

A pure function is a function whose output result depends only on its input data, and its execution has no side effect, like, for example, updating a global variable. Given an input value, a pure function always returns the same result.

A pure component is a component that acts like a pure function. This means that, given the same initial conditions, it always renders the same output.

It is very important to keep the render() method a pure function. This avoids weird bugs, as we will see in the next chapter.

Once we have defined our component, we can use it as a React element inside any other React component. For example, we know that the React application itself is already a React component. Let's recall the code generated by the create-react-app tool in the App.js file:

```
import React, { Component } from 'react';
import logo from './logo.svg';
import './App.css';

class App extends Component {
  render() {
    return (
      <div className="App">
        <header className="App-header">
          <img src={logo} className="App-logo" alt="logo" />
          <h1 className="App-title">Welcome to React</h1>
        </header>
        <p className="App-intro">
          To get started, edit <code>src/App.js</code> and save to reload.
        </p>
      </div>
    );
  }
}

export default App;
```

We can see that this code has the same structure as the `Catalog` component that we defined. Let's change this code in order to use our component inside of the `App` component:

```
import React, { Component } from 'react';
import './App.css';
import Catalog from './Catalog';

class App extends Component {
  render() {
    return (
      <div className="App">
        <header className="App-header">
          <h1 className="App-title">The Catalog App</h1>
        </header>
        <Catalog />
      </div>
    );
  }
}

export default App;
```

We simplified the code by removing some of the automatically generated markup. We then imported the `Catalog` component, and put the `<Catalog />` element inside the `<div>` element returned by the app's `render()` method.

Building Our First React Component

The following steps open the existing project, `my-shop-01`, in order to show the result of the previous code changes:

1. Open a console window
2. Move to the `my-shop-1` folder
3. Run `npm install`
4. Run `npm start`

The following is an example of what we will see in a browser window:

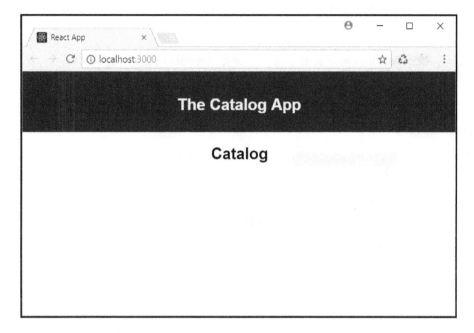

We have built our first React component, and we can see it in action!

Managing Styles

Perhaps you have noticed that we have an import statement concerning a CSS file in the App component module:

```
import React, { Component } from 'react';
import './App.css';
import Catalog from './Catalog';
```

This may seem a bit strange, since `import` statements should only work for JavaScript code. However, thanks to the development environment provided by `create-react-app`, we can use the same syntax, even for CSS files. This allows us to use the classes and other CSS definitions defined in `App.css` in our component, keeping component-specific styles close to the component definition itself. For example, if we want our `Catalog` component to have the title in red, we can proceed as shown next.

Adding CSS

We will now change the content of the existing project, `my-shop-01`, in order to add some CSS code and show the catalog title in red:

1. Open a console window.
2. Move to the `my-shop-1/src` folder.
3. Create a file, `Catalog.css`, and add the following code:

   ```
   h2 { color: red }
   ```

4. Open the `Catalog.js` file and add the statement to import the `Catalog.css` module, as shown here:

   ```
   import React from 'react';
   import './Catalog.css';

   class Catalog extends React.Component {
     render() {
       return <div><h2>Catalog</h2></div>;
     }
   }
   export default Catalog;
   ```

5. Run `npm start` and look at the result.

You can find a project ready in the `my-shop-02` folder at `Code/Chapter-2`.

The browser will show the **Catalog** title in red:

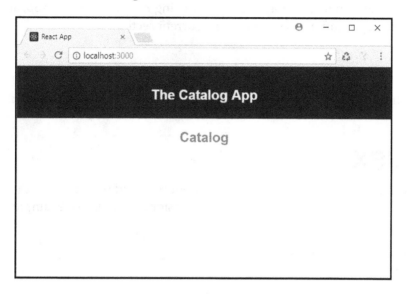

The CSS import is not a React feature, and it is not required by React. It is a convenience provided by the development environment, built by create-react-app. In particular, this feature is provided by **webpack**, one of the most frequently used bundlers and module loaders. You should take this aspect into account when you want to migrate the application into a development environment not based on webpack.

Activity: Defining a Shopping Cart

Scenario

We need a shopping cart for our e-shop.

Aim

The aim of this activity is to start using React to define a component.

Steps for Completion

1. We should define a React component that acts as the basis of a shopping cart
2. It should be a component that simply shows the string Cart

Create a new React application by using `create-react-app`, and change the application, as shown in the current section.

Solution

A possible solution is the one contained in the `my-cart-01` folder at `Code/Chapter-2/`.

Using JSX

In previous examples, we defined the visual output returned by the `render()` method of a component by using an HTML-like markup expression. Let's see, for example, the definition of the `Catalog` component:

```
import React from 'react';
import './Catalog.css';

class Catalog extends React.Component {
  render() {
    return <div><h2>Catalog</h2></div>;
  }
}

export default Catalog;
```

The markup expression is not using JavaScript syntax, but it is included inside of a JavaScript code snippet. Why do we mix HTML and JavaScript syntaxes? How is that possible?

Let's start by saying that the HTML-like language describing the React component's visual output is called **JSX**. This language extends JavaScript with XML expressions in order to simplify the creation of HTML elements within JavaScript code. You may think of it as a sort of `document.write("...")`, but much more powerful. In fact, when building a React application, the JSX markup is pre-processed by a specific parser, in order to produce pure JavaScript code. So, we can exploit the simplicity of using a declarative markup language that will automatically be converted into optimized JavaScript code.

As previously mentioned, a JSX expression creates a React element, which is the counterpart of an HTML element. From a syntactical point of view, a JSX expression is a single markup item with any nested elements. So, the following is a valid JSX expression:

```
<div><h2>Catalog</h2></div>
```

The following is not a valid JSX expression, since it contains two markup items:

```
<div><h2>Catalog</h2></div>
<div><img src="image.png" /></div>
```

> JSX expressions are XML fragments, so they are compliant with XML syntax rules. This means that, among other things, the markup is case-sensitive, and all of the tags must be closed.
>
> For example, the following JSX expression is not valid:
> ```
> <img src="image.png">
> ```
>
> Its valid version is the following:
> ```
> <img src="image.png"/>
> ```

We can assign a JSX expression to a variable, as in the following example:

```
import React from 'react';
import './Catalog.css';

class Catalog extends React.Component {
  render() {
    let output = <div><h2>Catalog</h2></div>;
    return output;
  }
}

export default Catalog;
```

We can also embed any JavaScript expression inside of a JSX expression by wrapping it in curly braces, as shown in the following example:

```
import React from 'react';
import './Catalog.css';

class Catalog extends React.Component {
  render() {
    let title = "Catalog";
    return <div><h2>{title}</h2></div>;
  }
}
export default Catalog;
```

Of course, the JavaScript expression can be as complex as we need it to be, like in the following component definition:

```
import React from 'react';
import './Catalog.css';

class Catalog extends React.Component {
  render() {
    let title = "The Catalog of today " + new Date().toDateString();
    return <div><h2>{title}</h2></div>;
  }
}

export default Catalog;
```

In addition to optimizing output rendering, JSX also provides support to prevent injection attacks. In fact, any value embedded in a JSX expression escapes before being rendered. This, for example, prevents malicious code from being inserted by a user's input.

A common use of a combination of JavaScript and JSX expressions is called **conditional rendering**; that is, a technique that allows you to generate a JSX expression based on some Boolean conditions. Consider the following example:

```
import React from 'react';
import './Message.css';

class Message extends React.Component {
  render() {
    let message;
    let today = new Date().getDay();

    if (today == 0) {
      message = <div className="sorry">We are closed on Sunday...</div>;
    } else {
      message = <div className="happy">How can we help you?</div>
    }
    return message;
  }
}

export default Message;
```

In the preceding example, the `render()` method returns one message or another, according to the current day of the week. This causes the generation of a React element with a different message and CSS class, but we could even return a completely different markup.

You can put a JSX expression in multiple lines, as in the following:

```
import React from 'react';
import './Catalog.css';

class Catalog extends React.Component {
  render() {
    let title = "Catalog";

    return <div>
      <h2>{title}</h2>
    </div>;
  }
}


export default Catalog;
```

> It is very important when returning a JSX expression to start it in the same line of the `return` statement, as in the previous example. If you want to start the JSX expression on a new line, you need to enclose it in round brackets and put the left bracket on the same line as the `return` statement, as in the following example:
> ```
> return (
>   
>     <h2>Catalog</h2>
>   );
> ```

You can put comments inside of a JSX expression by using the JavaScript syntax wrapped in curly brackets. The following is an example of a JSX expression with comments:

```
<div>
  <h2>Catalog</h2>
  {//This is a comment}
  {/* This is a comment, too */}
</div>;
```

JSX tags match HTML tags, which is why we can use the whole HTML syntax to define JSX elements. However, there are a few restrictions:

- All HTML tags are in lowercase
- You need to use `className` instead of the `class` attribute
- You need to use `htmlFor` instead of the `for` attribute

The following example shows the use of the `className` attribute instead of `class`:

```
<div className="catalog-style">
  <h2>Catalog</h2>
</div>;
```

 JSX uses the `className` and `htmlFor` attributes instead of `class` and `for` because as JSX expressions are inside JavaScript, `class` and `for` could clash with the corresponding reserved keywords.

Activity: Translating HTML into JSX

Scenario

The Graphics department has provided you with an HTML snippet, and you need to translate it into JSX in order to create a React component.

Aim

The aim of this activity is to understand the difference between HTML and JSX.

Steps for Completion

1. Open the `Code02.txt` file
2. Transform the HTML code it contains into JSX

Solution

A possible solution is the one contained in the `activity-b.html` file at `Code/Chapter-2/`.

Composing Components

When defining React components, we can use them as the children of another component by using that component as a React element. We already saw this when we included the `Catalog` component inside of the `App` component, but let's analyze this composition further.

Combining Components

We will now see how to combine components in order to create new, complex components:

1. Open the `src/ProductList.js` file in the `my-shop-03` folder
2. Follow the text until the end of the section

Let's consider the following component:

```
import React from 'react';
class ProductList extends React.Component {
  render() {
    return <ul>
      <li>
        <h3>Traditional Merlot</h3>
        <p>A bottle of middle weight wine, lower in tannins (smoother),
          with a more red-fruited flavor profile.</p>
      </li>
      <li>
        <h3>Classic Chianti</h3>
        <p>A medium-bodied wine characterized by a marvelous freshness with
          a lingering, fruity finish</p>
      </li>
      <li>
        <h3>Chardonnay</h3>
        <p>A dry full-bodied white wine with spicy, bourbon-y notes in an
          elegant bottle</p>
      </li>
      <li>
        <h3>Brunello di Montalcino</h3>
        <p>A bottle red wine with exceptionally bold fruit flavors,
          high tannin, and high acidity</p>
      </li>
    </ul>;
  }
}
export default ProductList;
```

This component defines a list of wines, names, and descriptions.

We want to integrate our `Catalog` component with the wine list. Since we have created the `ProductList` component, we can use it as a tag in the JSX markup of the `Catalog` component, as shown here:

```
import React from 'react';
import ProductList from './ProductList';

class Catalog extends React.Component {
  render() {
    return <div>
      <h2>Catalog</h2>
      <ProductList />
    </div>;
  }
}

export default Catalog;
```

As you can see, we simply imported the `ProductList` component in order to make it available inside the `Catalog` component's module, and we used the `ProductList` tag where we wanted the wine list to appear.

Run `npm start` to launch the application. The resulting page will look like this:

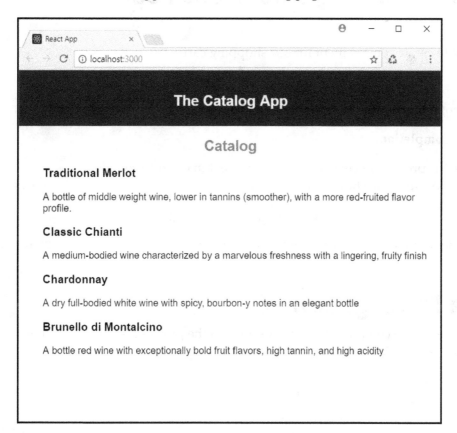

 We said that the HTML tags in JSX expressions should always be in lowercase. However, we used the `ProductList` tag in Pascal case.

Tags corresponding to components must follow the case used in the class definition, and by convention, component class names use Pascal case, even though it is not required by React.

The ease of composing React components makes it very simple to create user interfaces, following the guidelines provided in the previous chapter. We can decompose a page layout into a hierarchical set of components, each one consisting of other components. This approach allows us to focus on the behavior of a single component, and promotes its reusability.

Activity: Defining a Composed Cart

Scenario

We want to create some content for our shopping cart.

Aim

The aim of this activity is to compose React components.

Step for Completion

Integrate the previously created `Cart` component in order to contain a `CartList` component, showing two items.

Solution

A possible solution is the one contained in the `my-cart-02` folder at `Code/Chapter-2/`.

Data Propagation

The `ProductList` component that we defined in the previous section is impractical. Let's take a look at it again:

```
import React from 'react';
import './ProductList.css';

class ProductList extends React.Component {
  render() {
    return <ul>
      <li>
        <h3>Traditional Merlot</h3>
        <p>A bottle of middle weight wine, lower in tannins (smoother),
          with a more red-fruited flavor profile.</p>
      </li>
      <li>
        <h3>Classic Chianti</h3>
        <p>A medium-bodied wine characterized by a marvelous freshness with
          a lingering, fruity finish</p>
      </li>
      <li>
        <h3>Chardonnay</h3>
        <p>A dry full-bodied white wine with spicy, bourbon-y notes in an
          elegant bottle</p>
      </li>
```

```
      <li>
        <h3>Brunello di Montalcino</h3>
        <p>A bottle of red wine with exceptionally bold fruit flavors, high
          tannin, and high acidity</p>
      </li>
      </ul>;
    }
  }

  export default ProductList;
```

The list items are all defined as JSX markup, so if you need to change the
graphical appearance of the catalog's product, you need to change all of the occurrences
of each `<li>` element.

We can make a better implementation by going further in the user interface decomposition.
We can consider each list item as a component, and the `Product` component as the one
defined by the following code:

```
import React from 'react';

class Product extends React.Component {
  render() {
    return <li>
      <h3>Product name</h3>
      <p>Product description</p>
    </li>;
  }
}

export default Product;
```

This code acts as a template for each list item, so that we can build our product
list dynamically, as follows:

```
import React from 'react';
import './ProductList.css';
import Product from './Product';

class ProductList extends React.Component {
  render() {
    let products = [
      {code:"P01", name: "Traditional Merlot", description: "A bottle
       of middle weight wine, lower in tannins (smoother), with a
       more red-fruited flavor profile."},
      {code:"P02", name: "Classic Chianti", description: "A medium-bodied
       wine characterized by a marvelous freshness with a lingering,
```

```
          fruity finish"},
       {code:"P03", name: "Chardonnay", description: "A dry full-bodied
        white wine with spicy, bourbon-y notes in an elegant bottle"},
       {code:"P04", name: "Brunello di Montalcino", description: "A bottle
        of red wine with exceptionally bold fruit flavors, high tannin,
        and high acidity"}
    ];
    let productComponents = [];

    for (let product of products) {
      productComponents.push(<Product/>);
    }
    return <ul>{productComponents}</ul>;
  }
}


export default ProductList;
```

We can see the definition of an array of objects, `products`, containing the relevant data for each product. The second array, `productComponents`, will contain the list of React components created by merging product data with the `Product` component's markup. The `for` loop is intended to perform such merging. Finally, the resulting `productComponents` array, surrounded by the `<ul>` element, will be returned.

Even if the code structure appears to be correct, the result will not be as expected. In fact, we will obtain a list of items with the fixed names and descriptions that we put in the `Product` component definition. In other words, the merge between data and component definition didn't happen.

Actually, we need a way to pass the data of each product to the `Component` class. Let's think of React components as plain JavaScript functions. They may be implemented as functions returning React elements, and, as with any function, components may have data input. Such data input is passed through JSX attributes, and is accessible inside of a component through a special object called **props**. Let's change the `ProductList` component's code in order to pass data through JSX attributes:

```
import React from 'react';
import Product from './Product';

class ProductList extends React.Component {
  render() {
    let products = [
      {code:"P01", name: "Traditional Merlot", description: "A bottle
       of middle weight wine, lower in tannins (smoother), with a
       more red-fruited flavor profile."},
      {code:"P02", name: "Classic Chianti", description: "A medium-bodied
```

```
        wine characterized by a marvelous freshness with a lingering,
        fruity finish"},
      {code:"P03", name: "Chardonnay", description: "A dry full-bodied
        white wine with spicy, bourbon-y notes in an elegant bottle"},
      {code:"P04", name: "Brunello di Montalcino", description: "A bottle
        of red wine with exceptionally bold fruit flavors, high tannin,
        and high acidity"}
    ];

    let productComponents = [];

    for (let product of products) {
      productComponents.push(<Product
      item={product}/>);
    }

    return <ul>{productComponents}</ul>;
  }
}

export default ProductList;
```

We added an item attribute to the <Product> tag and assigned a single object from the products array to it. This allows us to pass the data of each product to the Product component.

On the other hand, we modify the Product component's code in order to receive and manage the passed data:

```
import React from 'react';

class Product extends React.Component {
  render() {
    return <li>
      <h3>{this.props.item.name}</h3>
      <p>{this.props.item.description}</p>
    </li>;
  }
}

export default Product;
```

 You can find a project ready in the my-shop-04 folder at Code/Chapter-2/.

Every React component has a `props` property. The purpose of this property is to collect data input passed to the component itself. Whenever a JSX attribute is attached to a React element, a property with the same name is attached to the `props` object. So, we can access the passed data by using the attached property. In our example, we found the product data passed via the `item` attribute mapped to the `this.props.item` property.

 `props` are immutable; that is, they are read-only properties.

This new implementation allows the catalog to be shown as before, but makes graphical markup independent from a product's data.

In a component hierarchy, data propagation is very important. It allows us to think about components as functions with inputs and outputs. In addition, the immutability of `props` allows us to think of components as pure functions, which are functions that have no side effects (since they don't change their input data). We can think of data passing from one component to another as a **unidirectional data flow**, from the parent component toward the child components. This gives us a more controllable system.

The following diagram shows how we would imagine the data propagation in a component hierarchy, ideally:

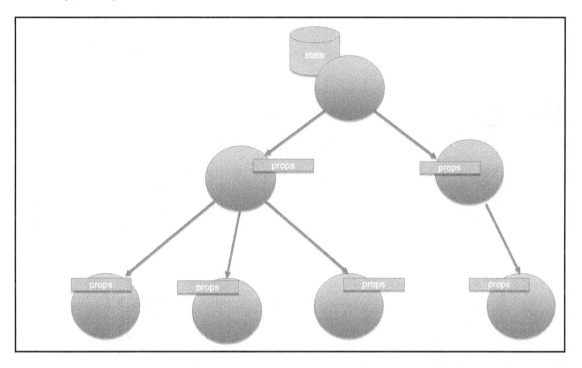

A change in the state causes a data propagation toward the child components through the props property.

Activity: Creating a Cart Item Component

Scenario

We want to make the CartList component a dynamic component, so that it can adapt its content to received data.

Aim

The aim of this activity is to compose React components and pass data between them.

Steps for Completion

1. Create a CartItem component showing the name of an item.

2. Change the previously created `CartList` component so that it is dynamically composed of `CartItem` instances, based on an `items` array.

Solution

A possible solution is the one contained in the `my-cart-03` folder at `Code/Chapter-2`.

Managing the Internal State

Components have the ability to store data that can change over time.

When a component shows data that can change over time, we want changes to be shown as soon as possible. For example, consider the `ProductList` component: it shows a list of products contained in the `products` array. If a new product is added to the array, we want it to be shown immediately. React provides a mechanism to support the automatic rendering of a component when data changes. Such a mechanism is based on the concept of **state**.

React `state` is a property that represents data that changes over time. Every component supports the `state` property, but it should be used carefully.

Again, consider the `ProductList` component:

```
import React from 'react';
import Product from './Product';

class ProductList extends React.Component {
  render() {
    let products = [
      {code:"P01", name: "Traditional Merlot", description: "A bottle
       of middle weight wine, lower in tannins (smoother), with a more
       red-fruited flavor profile."},
      {code:"P02", name: "Classic Chianti", description: "A medium-bodied
       wine characterized by a marvelous freshness with a lingering,
       fruity finish"},
      {code:"P03", name: "Chardonnay", description: "A dry full-bodied
       white wine with spicy, bourbon-y notes in an elegant bottle"},
      {code:"P04", name: "Brunello di Montalcino", description: "A bottle
       of red wine with exceptionally bold fruit flavors, high tannin,
       and high acidity"}
    ];
```

```
    let productComponents = [];

    for (let product of products) {
      productComponents.push(<Product item={product}/>);
    }
    return <ul>{productComponents}</ul>;
  }
}

export default ProductList;
```

From a practical point of view, it is not so useful. It shows a hardcoded list of products. If we want to add a new product, we need to make changes to the component source code.

In a real-world scenario, we want to keep the component's code independent from the product data. For example, we would get product data by making an HTTP request to the web server. In this case, the `products` array would represent data that changes over time: initially an empty array, it would then be filled with product data received from the server, and it could be changed again by subsequent requests to the server.

Components that store data that can change over time are said to be **stateful components**. A stateful component stores the state in the `this.state` property. To inform a component that the state has changed, you must use the `setState()` method. This method sets a new state for the component; it does not update it. Changes to the state trigger the component's rendering; that is, the automatic execution of the `render()` method.

Let's see how to manage the state by changing the `ProductList` component definition:

```
import React from 'react';
import Product from './Product';

class ProductList extends React.Component {
  constructor() {
    super();
    this.state = { products: [] };
    fetch("products.json")
      .then(response => response.json())
      .then(json => {this.setState({products: json})})
      .catch(error => console.log(error));
  }

  render() {
    let productComponents = [];

    for (let product of this.state.products) {
```

```
            productComponents.push(<Product item={product}/>);
        }
        return <ul>{productComponents}</ul>;
    }
}
export default ProductList;
```

We added the constructor to the component. The constructor runs the superclass constructor and sets the initial state of the component to an object with the `products` property as an empty array.

Then, send a GET HTTP request to the server via `fetch()`. Since the request is asynchronous, the initial rendering of the component will be an empty list of products.

 State initialization is the only case where you can assign a value to the `this.state` property without using `setState()`.

When the HTTP response is received, it is used to change the component's state with `setState()`. This state change causes the automatic execution of `render()`, which will show the list of products received from the server.

Now that we know how to manage the component's state, here are a couple of things to remember when using the `setState()` method:

- `setState()` merges new data with old data already contained in the state, and overwrites the previous state
- `setState()` triggers the execution of the `render()` method, so you should never call `render()` explicitly

Component state management appears to be very simple. However, it is easy to get in trouble when deciding what should be considered state and which component should be stateful.

Here is some advice about state:

- State should contain the minimum data needed to represent data that can change over time in your UI; any information that can be derived from this minimal data should be computed inside the `render()` method
- State should be avoided as much as possible, since it adds complexity to a component
- Stateful components should be located high up in the component hierarchy of a UI

We can consider the last piece of advice a consequence of the second piece of advice. If we should restrict the usage of state, we should reduce the number of stateful components. So, it is a good rule to assign the role of stateful component to components that are the root of a component hierarchy in a user interface. Do you remember the classification of components into presentational and container components, which we discussed in the previous chapter? In general, container components are good candidates for stateful components.

In our example application, we assigned the role of a stateful component to the ProductList component. Even if it is a container component, it is not the highest in the component hierarchy of the application. Maybe this role would be more appropriate for the Catalog component. In this case, we should move the logic of getting data inside of the Catalog component, as shown in the following code:

```
import React from 'react';
import './Catalog.css';
import ProductList from './ProductList';

class Catalog extends React.Component {
  constructor() {
    super();
    this.state = { products: [] };

    fetch("products.json")
      .then(response => response.json())
      .then(json => {this.setState({products: json})})
      .catch(error => console.log(error));
  }
  render() {
    return <div><h2>Wine Catalog</h2><ProductList
      items={this.state.products}/></div>;
  }
}

export default Catalog;
```

 You can find a project ready in the my-shop-05 folder at Code/Chapter-2.

Activity: Adding State Management to the Cart Component

Scenario

In order to make the `Cart` component production ready, we add state management and dynamic data loading.

Aim

The aim of this activity is to become familiar with component state management.

Step for Completion

Change the previously created `Cart` component to add state management, so that data is loaded via HTTP requests, and the contents of the cart is automatically updated.

Solution

A possible solution is the one contained in the `my-cart-04` folder at `Code/Chapter-2/`.

Summary

In this chapter, we started to create React components and explored their basic features. In particular, we:

- Learned how to define a component as a class derived from `React.Component`, and how to import specific CSS styles
- Explored the syntax of JSX, which allows us to quickly define the graphical aspect of a component and use React components that were defined elsewhere
- Combined React components in order to build other components
- Used state management features so that React components automatically update their visual representation when data changes

In the next chapter, we will analyze how to manage user interaction with a React-based application; in other words, how to capture events and make a UI react to those events.

3
Managing User Interactivity

In this chapter, we are going to learn how to manage the events generated by a user's interaction with the components of a React-based user interface. We will explore the events that are triggered during the lifecycle of a React component, and will learn how to exploit them in order to create efficient components. Finally, we will use the React Router library to allow easy navigation between the different views implemented by components.

By the end of this chapter, you will be able to:

- Handle events generated by user interaction
- Change a component's state on event triggering
- Use a component's lifecycle events for a better user experience
- Configure routing to allow navigation through components

Managing User Interaction

Any web application requires interaction between the user and the **user interface** (**UI**). An application without interaction is not a true application; interactivity is a basic requirement.

The application that we built in the previous chapter does not allow interaction. It simply shows data, and the user cannot do anything with it (apart from look at it).

Suppose that we want to introduce a little interaction into the catalog application that we started building in the previous chapter. For example, perhaps we want to show an alert with the price of the product when the user clicks on the product area.

Provided that the product data includes the price, as in the following JSON object:

```
[
  {"code":"P01",
   "name": "Traditional Merlot",
   "description": "A bottle of middle weight wine, lower in tannins
      (smoother), with a more red-fruited flavor profile.",
```

```
      "price": 4.5, "selected": false},
    {"code":"P02",
     "name": "Classiç Chianti",
     "description": "A medium-bodied wine characterized by a marvelous
         freshness with a lingering, fruity finish",
     "price": 5.3, "selected": false},
    {"code":"P03",
     "name": "Chardonnay",
     "description": "A dry full-bodied white wine with spicy,
         bourbon-y notes in an elegant bottle",
     "price": 4.0, "selected": false},
    {"code":"P04",
     "name": "Brunello di Montalcino",
     "description": "A bottle of red wine with exceptionally bold fruit
         flavors, high tannin, and high acidity",
     "price": 7.5, "selected": false}
  ]
```

We can implement this behavior as follows:

```
import React from 'react';

class Product extends React.Component {
  showPrice() {
    alert(this.props.item.price);
  }

  render() {
    return <li onClick={() => this.showPrice()}>
      <h3>{this.props.item.name}</h3>
      <p>{this.props.item.description}</p>
    </li>;
  }
}

export default Product;
```

Let's analyze the component's code and highlight the differences with respect to the previous version.

First of all, we added the showPrice() method, showing the price of the current product instance via an alert. This method is invoked inside of an arrow function assigned to the onClick attribute of the <li> tag.

These simple changes allow the Product component to capture the click event and execute the showPrice() method.

We'll now open the existing project, `my-shop-01`, in order to show the result of the previous code changes:

1. Open a console window
2. Move to the `my-shop-01` folder
3. Run `npm install`
4. Run `npm start`

The result of clicking on a product is shown in the following screenshot:

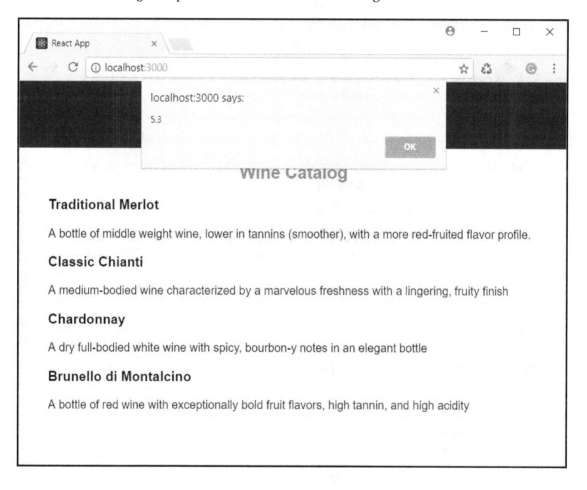

HTML Events versus React Events

As we can see, the React approach to handling events is very similar to classic event management within HTML. However, there are some subtle differences to take into account.

HTML events are named using lowercase, while JSX events use camelCase. For example, in HTML, you should use the following syntax:

```
<li onclick="...">...</li>
```

But in JSX, you use this syntax:

```
<li onClick=...>...</li>
```

In HTML, you assign a string representing the invocation of a function, while in JSX, you assign a function, which is shown as follows:

```
<li onclick="showPrice()">...</li>
<li onClick={showPrice}>...</li>
```

Of course, you can assign any JavaScript expression returning or representing a function, like the one shown in the following example:

```
<li onClick={() => this.showPrice()}>
```

Finally, you can prevent the default behavior of most HTML events by returning `false`, while in JSX events, you need to explicitly call `preventDefault`. The following is a typical example:

```
<a href="#" onClick={(e) => { e.preventDefault();
console.log("Clicked");}}>Click</a>
```

Event Handlers and the this Keyword

In the preceding example of defining a `Product` component, we assigned an arrow function to the `onClick` attribute, instead of the simple `showPrice()` method. This was not simply a matter of preference. It was necessary because we used the `this` keyword inside the `showPrice()` method.

In fact, when the event handler executes, the `this` keyword is no longer bound to the `Product` class, since it is asynchronously executed in a different context. This behavior does not depend on React, but on how JavaScript works.

In order to bind the method to the current class, we have a few options:

1. Use an arrow function and invoke the method inside its body, as shown in the following example:

   ```
   <li onClick={() => this.showPrice()}>
   ```

2. Use the `bind()` method to bind the method to the current class context, as shown in the following example:

   ```
   <li onClick={this.showPrice.bind(this)}>
   ```

3. You can use `bind()` in the class constructor instead of using it inline when assigning the method to the event attribute. The following is an example of this approach:

   ```
   constructor() {
   this.showPrice = this.showPrice.bind(this);
   }
   ...
   <li onClick={this.showPrice}>
   ```

Changing the State

The event management example that we looked at is very simple, but it only shows the basics of React event management. This example does not involve the state, and its management is straightforward. In many real-world cases, an event causes changes to the application's state, and that means changes to the component's state.

Suppose that, for example, you want to allow the selecting of products from the catalog. To do so, we add the `selected` property to each product object, as shown in the following array:

```
[
  {"code":"P01",
   "name": "Traditional Merlot",
   "description": "A bottle of middle weight wine, lower in tannins
      (smoother), with a more red-fruited flavor profile.",
   "price": 4.5, "selected": false},
  {"code":"P02",
   "name": "Classic Chianti",
   "description": "A medium-bodied wine characterized by a marvelous
      freshness with a lingering, fruity finish",
   "price": 5.3, "selected": false},
  {"code":"P03",
```

```
      "name": "Chardonnay",
      "description": "A dry full-bodied white wine with spicy, bourbon-y
         notes in an elegant bottle",
      "price": 4.0, "selected": false},
    {"code":"P04",
      "name": "Brunello di Montalcino",
      "description": "A bottle of red wine with exceptionally bold fruit
         flavors, high tannin, and high acidity",
      "price": 7.5, "selected": false}
  ]
```

When the user clicks on the product area, the value of the selected property is toggled and the background color of the area changes. The following code snippet shows the new version of the Product component:

```
import React from 'react';
import './Product.css'

class Product extends React.Component {
  select() {
    this.props.item.selected = !this.props.item.selected;
  }
  render() {
    let classToApply = this.props.item.selected? "selected": "";
    return <li onClick={() => this.select()} className={classToApply}>
             <h3>{this.props.item.name}</h3>
             <p>{this.props.item.description}</p>
           </li>;
  }
}

export default Product;
```

The select() method toggles the value of the selected property, while in the rendering method, we calculate the name of the class to apply according to the value of the selected property. The resulting class name is then assigned to the className attribute.

Unexpectedly, this code is not working correctly. You can verify it by performing the following steps. We can open the existing project, my-shop-02, in order to see the results of the previous code. Follow these steps:

1. Open a console window
2. Move to the my-shop-02 folder
3. Run npm install
4. Run npm start

The code is not working as expected because the `select()` method does not change the component's state, so the `render()` method is not triggered. In addition, keep in mind that the `props` property is read-only, so any change to it has no effect.

The `Product` component is a stateless component, so we have no state to change here. The product's data comes from the `Catalog` root component via `props`. So, how can we change the `Catalog` component's state, starting from an event triggered at the `Product` component instance?

Specifically, how can a child component change the state of its parent component?

Actually, the child component has no opportunity to change the parent component's state, because in a React component hierarchy, data flows in a unidirectional way, from the parent towards the children. We illustrate this flow in the following diagram:

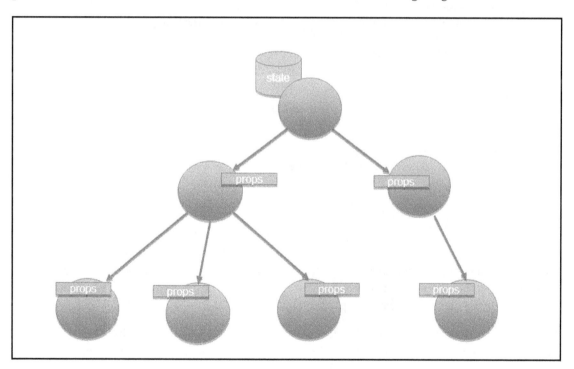

We cannot push data from the child to the parent. In order for a child component to change the state of a parent component, we need to get a method to act on that state. Since a component state is accessible only by the component itself, the parent component must provide that method to its children via the `props` property.

Consider the following code:

```
import React from 'react';
import './Catalog.css';
import ProductList from './ProductList';

class Catalog extends React.Component {
  constructor() {
    super();
    this.state = { products: [] };

    fetch("products.json")
      .then(response => response.json())
      .then(json => {this.setState({products: json})})
      .catch(error => console.log(error));
  }

  select(productCode) {
    let productList = this.state.products.map(function(p) {
      if (p.code === productCode) {
        p.selected = (!p.selected);
      }
      return p;
    });
    this.setState({products: productList});
  }
  render() {
    return <div><h2>Wine Catalog</h2><ProductList
      items={this.state.products} selectHandler={this.select}/></div>;
  }
}

export default Catalog;
```

The preceding code adds the select() method to the Catalog component. This method takes a product code as an input parameter, gets the product list from the component's state, and updates the selected property of the corresponding product. It then updates the component's state with the new product list.

The select() method is assigned to the new selectHandler attribute in the ProductList tag, so the corresponding component can access it through the props property.

The following code shows how this.props.selectHandler is passed from the ProductList component to the Product component via the selectHandler attribute:

```
import React from 'react';
import './ProductList.css';
import Product from './Product';

class ProductList extends React.Component {
  render() {
    let products = [];

    for (let product of this.props.items) {
      products.push(<Product item={product}
        selectHandler={this.props.selectHandler}/>);
    }
    return <ul>{products}</ul>;
  }
}

export default ProductList;
```

Finally, the `Product` component handles the `onClick` events by calling the `select()` method passed via the `this.props.selectHandler` property with the appropriate product code:

```
import React from 'react';
import './Product.css'

class Product extends React.Component {
  render() {
    let classToApply = this.props.item.selected? "selected": "";

    return <li onClick={() => this.props.selectHandler
    (this.props.item.code)} className={classToApply}>
      <h3>{this.props.item.name}</h3>
      <p>{this.props.item.description}</p>
    </li>
  }
}

export default Product;
```

We'll now open the existing project, `my-shop-03`, in order to see the results of the previous code. Follow these steps:

1. Open a console window
2. Move to the `my-shop-03` folder
3. Run `npm install`
4. Run `npm start`

We can conclude that an event on a child component triggers the execution of a parent component method passed via `props`. The method changes the parent's state, and the effect of this change is once again propagated to the children via `props`. The following diagram illustrates this behavior:

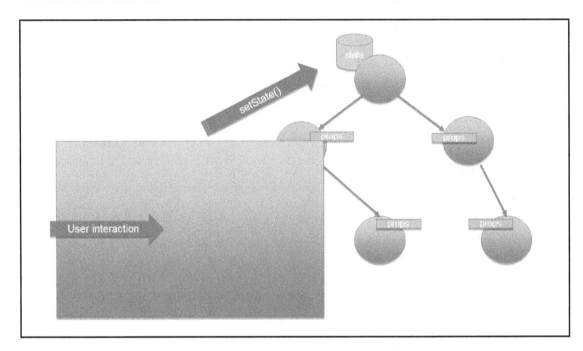

Activity: Adding Items to the Shopping Cart

Scenario

We want to allow the user to add items to the shopping cart by picking them from the product catalog.

Aim

The aim of this activity is to become familiar with event management in React.

Steps for Completion

1. Consider the existing project in the `my-cart-01` folder
2. Handle the click event of the `Product` component's **Add to cart** button in order to add that product to the cart

Solution

A possible solution is the one contained in the `my-cart-02` folder at `Code/Chapter-3/`.

Component Lifecycle Events

In a React application, components are created dynamically, according to the evolution of the application at runtime. A user's interaction starts a component's creation, its visualization, its updates on the screen, and its destruction.

So, components go through different phases during application execution: these phases represent their lifecycles.

React allows us to intercept and manage the phases of a component's lifecycle in a customized way, thanks to a set of events that we can handle by implementing specific methods.

Before analyzing a component's lifecycle events, we should highlight that the first step in creating a component is the execution of its constructor. Although it is not one of React's lifecycle phases, it is the first step of a component's life. During the component's constructor execution, the DOM is not available, and it is not possible to access any child component. The constructor execution is the right time to perform the initializations that don't concern graphic rendering or child manipulation.

After component creation, React will trigger a few events corresponding to the respective phases of the component's lifecycle. We can catch these events and handle them by implementing a few methods in our component. Consider the following method:

```
componentWillMount
```

This method is executed when the component is about to be inserted into the DOM. It is invoked once, just before the initial rendering occurs. Usually, this method is used to perform any initialization of the component not involving the DOM, such as initializing values for a component's properties or local variables.

 You can use the `setState()` method within `componentWillMount()`, but it will not trigger a re-render of the component, so use it carefully.

`componentWillReceiveProps` is the method invoked before rendering when a component receives new values from the parent via `props`. This method receives the new values as a parameter, and we can access the old values through `this.props`.

If we try to change the component state during the execution of this method, we will not trigger any additional rendering. Additionally, `componentWillReceiveProps()` is not to be invoked upon initial rendering.

The `shouldComponentUpdate` method should return a Boolean that states whether the component should be rendered (`true`) or not (`false`). If the method returns `false`, the next methods will not be invoked, including `render()`.

This has two parameters: `nextProps`, containing the new values for the `props`, and `nextState`, containing the new value of the component's state.

`componentWillUpdate` is invoked immediately before the `render()` method, so it is the last opportunity to perform some processing before updating the component.

 You cannot use `setState()` within an implementation of `shouldComponentUpdate()`.

`componentDidUpdate` is invoked immediately after rendering occurs, and during its execution, we can access the new version of the component in the DOM. The method has two parameters: the previous `props` and the previous state.

`componentDidMount` is called after the component is inserted into the DOM, and is invoked just once.

`componentWillUnmount` is called immediately before the component is removed from the DOM.

 You cannot use `setState()` during the execution of this method.

We can group the component lifecycle events into three main areas:

- **Mounting**: This `props` group contains the events related to DOM manipulation: `componentWillMount`, `componentDidMount`, and `componentWillUnmount`

- **Updating via props**: This group contains the events that are triggered when a component is updated via `props` passed by its parent, and it includes: `componentWillReceiveProps`, `shouldComponentUpdate`, `componentWillUpdate`, and `componentDidUpdate`

- **Updating via setState()**: In this group, we find the events triggered when a component is updated via `setState()`: `shouldComponentUpdate`, `componentWillUpdate`, and `componentDidUpdate`

The following diagram illustrates the event flow and highlights, with different colors, the three areas we just discussed:

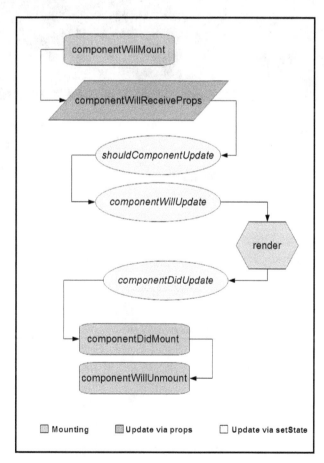

Activity: Showing the Quantity of Items Added to the Cart

Scenario

We want to avoid multiple occurrences of the same product in the cart. Rather, we want the cart to have a single occurrence of a product and its quantity, as shown in the following screenshot:

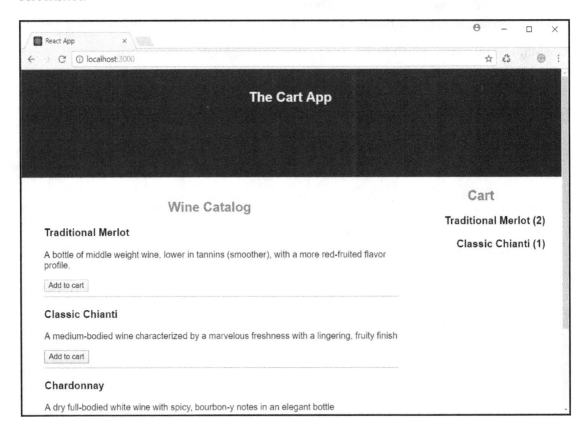

Aim

The aim of this activity is to exploit the lifecycle events of React components.

Steps for Completion

1. Utilize the project that was changed in the previous activity (or the existing project in the my-cart-02 folder).
2. Change the Cart component in order to show a list of non-duplicated products and their related number of occurrences.

Handle the componentWillReceiveProps event to prepare data for the internal state of the Cart component.

Solution

A possible solution is the one contained in the my-cart-03 folder at Code/Chapter-3.

Managing Routing

Modern web applications, based on the Single-Page Application model, can't do without the routing mechanism, a way to navigate among views while remaining on the same HTML page.

We can consider a view as a placeholder in the UI where we can dynamically render one component or another in an exclusive way. Let's try to clarify this concept with an example.

Suppose that we want to add a navigation bar to our *Wine Catalog* application. In its simplest implementation, we want to alternatively show the **Catalog** and an **About** section, providing some information about the application itself. The new UI will look like the following screenshot:

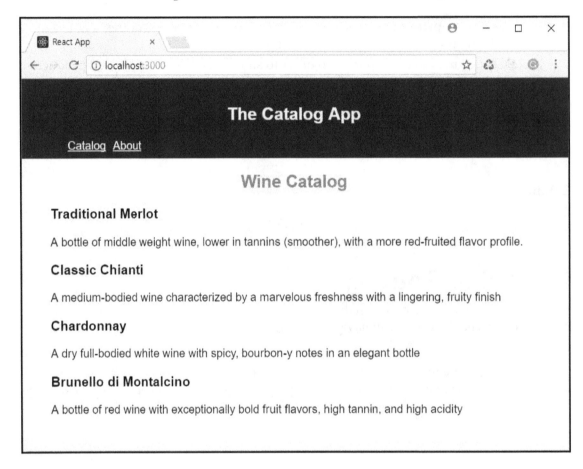

When clicking a menu item, we expect the main area to change, while the header remains the same. In this case, the main area will be the view in which we display the `Catalog` component or the `About` component, depending on the menu item we clicked on.

How can we implement the routing mechanism in React?

Installing React Router

We can enable routing in a React-based application by using **React Router**, a package that provides us with specific React components that allow us to set up a complete routing system.

We install that package in our application by typing the following command inside of the application's folder:

```
npm install --save react-router-dom
```

React Router provides three packages:

- react-router
- react-router-dom
- react-router-native

The first package provides the core routing components and functionalities. The second one provides specific components for the browser environment, and the third one supports react-native, an environment that maps React components to native mobile UI widgets. Both react-router-dom and react-router-native use react-router functionalities.

Using the Router

Once we have installed the React Router package in our environment, we need to use the provided components in our application.

The first thing we need to do is add routing capabilities to our application. We can do this by changing the code of the index.js file, as follows:

```
import React from 'react';
...
import { BrowserRouter } from 'react-router-dom'

ReactDOM.render(
  <BrowserRouter>
    <App />
  </BrowserRouter>
  , document.getElementById('root'));
registerServiceWorker();
```

We highlighted the main differences, with respect to the previous version of the code. As you can see, we imported the BrowserRouter component from the react-router-dom module and wrapped the App component inside of it.

By wrapping the `App` component, the `BrowserRouter` component enriches it with routing capabilities.

 This is a component composition hence we have called this as component wrapping.

Defining Views

Now, we need to create a view to display the `Catalog` component or the **About** page, as depicted in the following screenshot:

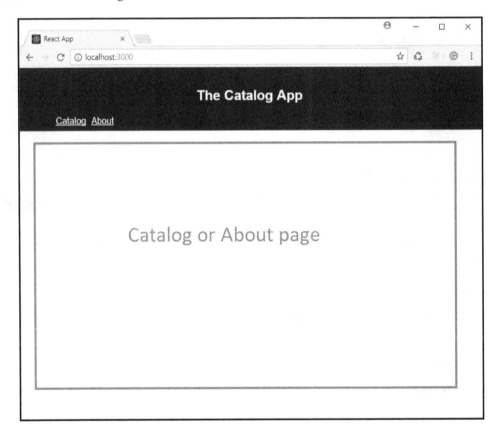

We can accomplish this by changing the `App.js` code, which is shown as follows:

```
import React, { Component } from 'react';
import './App.css';
import Catalog from './Catalog';
import About from './About';
import { Switch, Route } from 'react-router-dom'

class App extends Component {
  render() {
    return (
      <div className="App">
        <header className="App-header">
          <h1 className="App-title">The Catalog App</h1>
          <nav>
            <ul>
              <li><Link to='/'>Catalog</Link></li>
              <li><Link to='/about'>About</Link></li>
            </ul>
          </nav>
        </header>
        <Switch>
          <Route exact path='/' component={Catalog}/>
          <Route path='/about' component={About}/>
        </Switch>
      </div>
    );
  }
}

export default App;
```

We imported the `Switch` and `Route` components from the `react-router-dom` module, and used them in the JSX expression where the `Catalog` element once was.

The `Switch` component allows us to define a view, that is, the area inside of which we will toggle components. The `Route` components are used as child elements of `Switch`, and they allow us to map URLs to components. In our example, we are mapping the root URL (/) to the `Catalog` component and the `/about` URL to the `About` component. This means that when the `BrowserRouter` intercepts the request to move to one of these URLs, it will render the appropriate component inside of the view.

The navigation bar that allows us to display the catalog or the information about the application is implemented as follows:

```
import React, { Component } from 'react';
import './App.css';
```

```
import Catalog from './Catalog';
import About from './About';
import { Switch, Route, Link } from 'react-router-dom'

class App extends Component {
  render() {
    return (
      <div className="App">
        <header className="App-header">
          <h1 className="App-title">The Catalog App</h1>
          <nav>
            <ul>
              <li><Link to='/'>Catalog</Link></li>
              <li><Link to='/about'>About</Link></li>
            </ul>
          </nav>
        </header>
        <Switch>
          <Route exact path='/' component={Catalog}/>
          <Route path='/about' component={About}/>
        </Switch>
      </div>
    );
  }
}

export default App;
```

Here, we added the import of a `Link` component and used it in the highlighted markup. The `Link` component allows us to create a hyperlink element that will be caught by the `BrowserRouter` component.

These changes add a working navigation bar to our application. You can see the result of these changes by performing the following steps.

We will open the existing project, `my-shop-04`, in order to show the results of the previous code:

1. Open a console window
2. Move to the `my-shop-04` folder
3. Run `npm install`
4. Run `npm start`

Some Notes About the Route Component

Notice that the Route component has the path attribute (which allows us to specify the URL to map) and the component attribute (which allows us to assign the component to render in the current view):

```
<Switch>
<Route exact path='/' component={Catalog}/>
<Route path='/about' component={About}/>
</Switch>
```

The path attribute is used by React Router to detect the component to render, as specified by the corresponding component attribute.

In the previous route mapping, if we click on a Link component associated with the /about URL, the route with the root (/) path will match the starting part of /about, and the Catalog component will be rendered.

When the user requests a URL by clicking on the Link component, the list of routes is scanned in order to find a path value that matches the starting part of the URL. The first matching value determines the component to render.

If we want a strict comparison between the path attribute's value and the URL, we need to specify the exact attribute, which is shown as follows:

```
<Switch>
<Route exact path='/' component={Catalog}/>
<Route path='/about' component={About}/>
</Switch>
```

This prevents any URL starting with / from being captured by the first route.

The component attribute of the Route component allows us to specify the component to render. Alternatively, we can use the render attribute to specify the invocation of a function returning a React element, as shown in the following example:

```
<Route path='/about' render={() => (<About data={someData}/>)}/>
```

This approach is similar to using the component attribute, but it may be useful for inline rendering and when we need to pass values to the element.

The `Route` component also allows us to specify the `children` attribute. As with `render`, we can assign a function to this attribute, but the elements returned by that function will *always* be rendered, regardless of whether the path matches or not.

Consider the following example:

```
<Switch>
<Route 'exact path='/' component={Catalog}/>
<Route path='/about' component={About }/>
<Route path='/footer' children={() => (<Footer />)}/>
</Switch>
```

The `Footer` component will always be rendered, even if the path `/footer` doesn't match.

Nested Views

In the preceding examples, we implemented view navigation in the `App` component by using the `Switch`, `Route`, and `Link` components provided by React Router. We can use these routing components inside of any other component so that we can build nested views and nested routes.

Let's try to illustrate this with an example. Suppose that we want to add a list of winemakers to our application. We can add a new item to the navigation bar that allows us to navigate to a page showing that list.

The following screenshot shows how the new layout will appear:

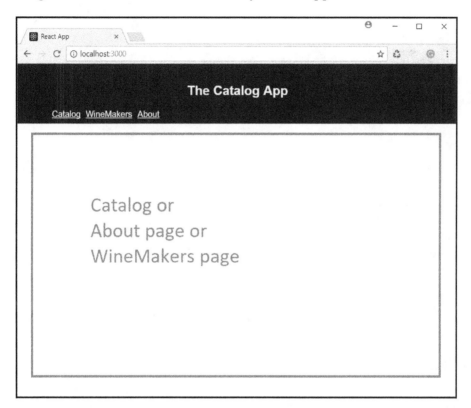

So, let's change the App component's JSX markup, as follows:

```
import React, { Component } from 'react';
import './App.css';
import Catalog from './Catalog';
import About from './About';
import WineMakers from './WineMakers';
import { Switch, Route, Link } from 'react-router-dom';

class App extends Component {
  render() {
    return (
      <div className="App">
        <header className="App-header">
          <h1 className="App-title">The Catalog App</h1>
          <nav>
            <ul>
              <li><Link to='/'>Catalog</Link></li>
```

```
                <li><Link to='/winemakers'>WineMakers</Link></li>
                <li><Link to='/about'>About</Link></li>
              </ul>
            </nav>
          </header>
          <Switch>
            <Route exact path='/' component={Catalog}/>
            <Route path='/winemakers' component={WineMakers}/>
            <Route path='/about' component={About}/>
          </Switch>
        </div>
      );
    }
  }

  export default App;
```

We imported the `WineMakers` component, defined a route that maps the `/winemakers` path to the new component, and added a link to navigate to it.

We can implement the list of winemakers as follows:

```
import React from 'react';
import WineMaker from './WineMaker';
import { Switch, Route, Link } from 'react-router-dom';

class WineMakers extends React.Component {
  renderWineMakersList() {
    return <ul>
  ...
        <Link to="/winemakers/WM2">Wine & Co</Link>
      </li>
    </ul>;
  }

  render() {
    return <Switch>
    ...

  export default WineMakers;
```

The `WineMakers` component has the `renderWineMakersList()` method that returns the React element implementing a list of links to each winemaker. This method is used as the value of the `render` attribute of the route matching the `/winemakers` path in the `render()` method of the component. The other routes get the path pointing to each specific winemaker and render the `WineMaker` component according to the identifier code.

You may notice that we are implementing a view in the `WineMakers` component that is shown inside of the view implemented in the `App` component. In other words, we implement nested views by composing components that implement views.

Path Parameters

The `render()` method of the `WineMakers` component implements the resulting view as follows:

```
render() {
  return <Switch>
    <Route exact path='/winemakers' render={this.renderWineMakersList}/>
    <Route path='/winemakers/WM1' render={() => (<WineMaker code='WM1'
/>}/>
    <Route path='/winemakers/WM2' render={() => (<WineMaker code='WM2'
/>}/>
  </Switch>;
}
```

This code is straightforward, and it works, but it forces us to add a new route whenever a new winemaker is added to our list.

We can avoid this by using `path` parameters, as in the following code:

```
render() {
  return <Switch>
    <Route exact path='/winemakers' render={this.renderWineMakersList}/>
    <Route path='/winemakers/:code' component={WineMaker}/>
  </Switch>;
}
```

As you can see, we can now use a single route pointing to a specific winemaker by specifying a `:code` parameter. The colon in the path expression indicates that the following portion of the URL is a variable value. You may also notice that we used the `component` attribute instead of the `render` attribute. In fact, in this case, we do not need to explicitly pass the winemaker's code to the `WineMaker` component. React Router does it for us, by providing a special object in the `props` property.

Let's take a look at the `WineMaker` component implementation:

```
import React from 'react';

class WineMaker extends React.Component {
  constructor() {
    super();
```

```
this.wineMakers = [
  {code: "WM1", name: "Wine & Wine", country: "Italy",
  description:"Wine & Wine produces an excellent Italian wine..."},

export default WineMaker;
```

In the component's constructor, we define the list of winemakers as an array of objects.

In the `render()` method, we look for the winemaker to display by comparing the `code` property of each `winemaker` object in the array with the `match.params.code` property provided by `this.props`.

 We have implemented the `winemakers` list as a property of the `WineMaker` component, and not as a property of the `state` object because since the list is embedded into the code and shouldn't change, we do not need to implement it as a `state` property. Remember that we only identify data that changes over time as a state.

The object we find is used to appropriately render the data about the `WineMaker`.

Generally, a React component reached via a route receives the `match` object in the `this.props` property. This object contains information about the matching path in the `Route` definition. In particular, the following properties of the `match` object are available:

- `params`: This is an object whose properties match the parameters in the path; that is, the dynamic parts, preceded by colons
- `isExact`: This is a Boolean indicating that the URL matches the path
- `path`: This is the string assigned to the `path` attribute of the selected route
- `url`: This is the URL that matches the route's path

We can see the final result by performing the following steps. We open the existing project, `my-shop-05`, in order to show the results of the previous code:

1. Open a console window
2. Move to the `my-shop-05` folder
3. Run `npm install`
4. Run `npm start`

Activity: Adding a View About Shipping Methods

Scenario

We want to add a section to our catalog app containing information about the available shipping methods.

Aim

The aim of this activity is to explore the components provided by React Routing.

Steps for Completion

1. Consider the project that was changed in the previous activity (or the existing project in the `my-cart-03` folder).
2. Create a `ShippingMethods` component, showing a list of available shipping methods, and a `ShippingMethod` component, showing the details of each shipping method, according to a code passed via `props` (available shipping methods include **Economic delivery** (**ECO**), **Standard delivery** (**STD**), and **Express delivery** (**EXP**)).
3. Create a navigation bar and a routing configuration that allow us to navigate through the `Catalog` and `Shipping` method views.

Solution

A possible solution is the one contained in the `my-cart-04` folder at `Code/Chapter-3`.

Summary

In this chapter, we learned how to manage user interaction. In particular, we have covered the following things:

- Managed events that don't involve changes to a component's state
- Handled events that involve changes to a component's state
- Explored the component lifecycle and learned how to customize each phase
- Used React Router's components to configure navigation between components

This chapter concludes the book. It provided the basics for understanding how React works and how to build React-based applications. We started with an introduction to React and then explored creating components in detail. We finished with a look at how to manage user interactivity with React.

Other Books You May Enjoy

If you enjoyed this book, you may be interested in these other books by Packt:

Full-Stack React Projects
Shama Hoque

ISBN: 978-1-78883-553-4

- Set up your development environment and develop a MERN application
- Implement user authentication and authorization using JSON Web Tokens
- Build a social media application by extending the basic MERN application
- Create an online marketplace application with shopping cart and Stripe payments
- Develop a media streaming application using MongoDB GridFS
- Implement server-side rendering with data to improve SEO
- Set up and use React 360 to develop user interfaces with VR capabilities
- Learn industry best practices to make MERN stack applications reliable and scalable

Progressive Web Apps with React
Scott Domes

ISBN: 978-1-78829-755-4

- Set up Webpack configuration, as well as get the development server running
- Learn basic Firebase configuration and deployment
- Create routes, manage multiple components, and learn how to use React Router v4 to manage the flow of data
- Use React lifecycle methods to load data
- Add a service worker to the app and learn how it works
- Use a service worker to send push notifications
- Configure Webpack to split up the JavaScript bundle and lazy load component files
- Learn how to use the web Cache API to use your app offline
- Audit PWAs with Google's Lighthouse

Leave a review - let other readers know what you think

Please share your thoughts on this book with others by leaving a review on the site that you bought it from. If you purchased the book from Amazon, please leave us an honest review on this book's Amazon page. This is vital so that other potential readers can see and use your unbiased opinion to make purchasing decisions, we can understand what our customers think about our products, and our authors can see your feedback on the title that they have worked with Packt to create. It will only take a few minutes of your time, but is valuable to other potential customers, our authors, and Packt. Thank you!

Index

www.ingramcontent.com/pod-product-compliance
Lightning Source LLC
Chambersburg PA
CBHW080541060326
40690CB00022B/5199